DPT

ALLEN COUNTY PUBLIC LIBRARY

3 1833 03074 5605

D0149361

j796.75
Dregni, Michael.
Motorcycle racing

9/97

ALLEN COUNTY PUBLIC LIBRARY
FORT WAYNE, INDIANA 46802

You may return this book to any location of
the Allen County Public Library.

DEMCO

Motorcycle Racing

Michael Dregni

Capstone Press

MINNEAPOLIS

Allen County Public Library
900 Webster Street
PO Box 2270
Fort Wayne, IN 46801-2270

Copyright © 1994 Capstone Press. All rights reserved. No part of this book may be reproduced in any form without written permission from the publisher.

Printed in the United States of America.

Capstone Press • 2440 Fernbrook Lane • Minneapolis, MN 55447

Editorial Director   John Coughlan
Managing Editor   John Martin
Copy Editor   Theresa Early
Editorial Assistant   Michelle Wood

Library of Congress Cataloging-in-Publication Data

Dregni, Michael, 1961-
    Motorcycle racing / Michael Dregni.
        p. cm. -- (Motorsports)
    Includes bibliographical references and index.
    ISBN 1-56065-207-1
    1. Motorcycle racing--Juvenile literature.
    [1. Motorcycle racing.]   I. Title.   II. Series.
    GV1060.D74   1994
    796.7'5--dc20   93-44569
                                                        CIP
                                                        AC

ISBN: 1-56065-207-1

99 98 97 96   8 7 6 5 4 3

Table of Contents

Chapter   1   Skills and Thrills 5

Chapter   2   Motorcycle Racing History..............7

Chapter   3   Today's Racing Motorcycles..........11

Chapter   4   The Race Is On! 13

Chapter   5   Safety Gear 19

Chapter   6   Dirt-Track Racing 23

Chapter   7   Motocross Racing 29

Chapter   8   Supercross Racing........................33

Chapter   9   Road Racing.................................37

Chapter 10   Drag Racing 41

Glossary 44

To Learn More...46

Index 47

Expert rider Chris Bense leads the pack during a motocross race.

Chapter 1

Skills and Thrills

A motorcycle race is a battle of speed and skill. It is fought through every lap from start to finish.

Drivers ride motorcycles with engines measuring from 125 cubic centimeters (cc) to 1500cc and more. Racers speed their machines over dirt or pavement. Some travel faster than 200 miles (322 kilometers) per hour. They lean into the turns to urge their machines toward the finish line.

Welcome to the exciting world of motorcycle racing!

The Daytona 200 motorcycle race, shown here in 1950, is still popular today.

Chapter 2

Motorcycle Racing History

Motorcycles have thrilled both riders and spectators for more than 100 years. The first motorcycle was built in 1885. Its frame was wood and it had a crude gasoline engine. Gottlieb Daimler built this pioneer cycle. Other models followed. A French model was powered by a steam engine like an old train locomotive!

Motordrome Boardtrack Racing

The first official motorcycle races in the

United States were held on bicycle-racing tracks called **velodromes**. These early tracks were built of wood with high, banked corners, shaped like a bowl. When motorcycles took over between 1908 and 1913, the tracks became known as "**motordromes**."

As the motorcycles raced, oil from their engines spilled onto the boards, making them slippery. The final race was the most dangerous—and most exciting for the fans.

Because of all the accidents, public officials ended boardtrack racing.

The first racing motorcycles in the United States were called Indians. They were built in 1901 by George Hendee and Oscar Hedstrom in Springfield, Massachusetts.

Their first motorcycle used a 288cc motor. It had only 2.25 **horsepower**. Its top speed was just 30 miles (48 kilometers) per hour.

Other early makers of motorcycles in the United States were Thor, Ace, Henderson, Excelsior, and Harley-Davidson.

Bobby Hill sits atop his 1953 Indian racing motorcycle.

10

3 1833 03074 5605

Chapter 3

Today's Racing Motorcycles

Modern racing motorcycles weigh much less than a car. But they can have as much horsepower. The combination of light weight and lots of horsepower can give a racing motorcycle quicker **acceleration** from the starting line than an Indianapolis 500 race car. A racing motorcycle's top speed can be over 200 miles (322 kilometers) per hour.

Over the years, many different types of motorcycles have been built. Each is used for a different type of racing.

Chapter 4

The Race Is On!

Although the types of motorcycles and tracks differ very much, the typical race is always pretty much the same.

Most motorcycle races begin when the race **steward** or referee waves a green flag. The riders gun their engines and blast off.

A Battle of Speed and Skill

When they turn, riders lean their motorcycles into the corners. In road racing, a rider's knee rubs the pavement. The rider hangs off the motorcycle to get every last bit of speed out of the cycle.

During a road race, the riders' knees actually scrape the pavement.

The race steward waves the checkered flag to signal the end of the race.

In dirt-track, motocross, and supercross racing, riders carve around the turns and balance with an outstretched leg. Thick-soled boots protect the riders' feet.

Racing for the Checkered Flag

No matter which type of race, it always comes down to the last push, when the **checkered flag** comes out.

Riders flick their motorcycles upright. They roll open the throttle to **WFO**, or **wide full open**. Riders lean forward to put their weight onto the front wheel, so they won't do wheelies.

The race steward waits at the finish line. The lead cycles dice it out. The riders are tucked in behind the handlebars to keep out of the wind.

They cross the finish line. The crowd leaps to its feet cheering. The steward waves the checkered flag, and the race is won.

Every motorcycle racer wears a full set of safety gear including riding leathers, gloves, boots, and a helmet.

Chapter 5

Safety Gear

Motorcycle racing is a dangerous sport. All riders must wear protective clothing. A full set of safety gear includes **riding leathers**, gloves, leather boots, and a helmet.

Riding Leathers

Riding pants for dirt-track, motocross, and supercross racing are called leathers. But they are not really made of leather. Most are made of a very tough nylon. They will protect the legs from the ground during a fall.

Racers put hard plastic knee, shin, and hip pads inside the pants for extra protection.

The Real Leathers

Calling road-racing pants *leathers* makes more sense. These pants *are* made of leather. They also protect the rider's legs from scrapes during a fall.

Besides being made of leather, road-racing pants have another major difference. On the outside of each knee is a skid plate. It is made of plastic or metal. It protects the racer's knee when it scrapes the pavement during turns.

In the past leathers were all black. Today, racers wear leathers in every color imaginable.

Gloves

All motorcycle racers wear sturdy gloves. They may be made of leather or nylon, or a combination of the two.

Boots

Motorcycle racers' feet need to be well protected. In dirt-track, motocross, and supercross, racers' feet are always at risk of being run over.

Boots are made of extra-thick cowhide. They have plastic and metal plates built into them.

Motocross racers wear knee-length boots. All other motorcycle racers use shorter boots that end at the shin.

Helmets

Helmets protect the most vulnerable part of a motorcycle racer's body–the head.

Helmets are made of fiberglass or plastic. The most popular style of helmet for motorcycle racing is the **full-face helmet**. It covers the whole head, the cheeks, and the chin.

Usually a clear, shatter-proof shield is attached to the front of the helmet. It protects the racer's eyes from wind, dirt, and debris.

Motocross and supercross racers do not use a shield. They protect their eyes with goggles. The goggles fit inside the helmet and are secured with a strap.

Top dirt-track racer Chris Carr in first place

Chapter 6

Dirt-Track Racing

At the same time as the motordromes developed, motorcycle racing started on horse-racing tracks. It was natural to hold races there because the tracks were already built.

The Track

Dirt tracks are simply made of dirt and do not have banked turns. Most dirt tracks are oval-shaped and are either .5 or 1 mile (.8 or 1.6 kilometers) long.

The loose dirt on the surface lets the riders slide around the flat turns.

The Cycles

In the early days of dirt-tracking, the motorcycles were no different from road-racing cycles. Today they are designed especially for dirt-track racing. They have large, 750cc engines and lightweight **chassis**.

Early rules did not allow brakes. They were considered a dangerous accessory. Brakes are used today, but only on the rear wheel.

The motorcycles that rule American dirt-track racing today are all Harley-Davidsons. The Harley XR-750 model of 1970–1993 has won more races than any other type of motorcycle.

The Race

On dirt tracks, riders hold one leg straight out to slide around the corners. Huge clouds of dust follow the riders around the tracks. Riders struggle for first place. They want to win the **purse**, or first-place prize money, but they also do not want to eat another motorcycle's dust.

Chris Carr demonstrates the technique of "broadsiding."

Dirt-track racing takes a special riding technique. Riders have to **broadside** their machines around flat turns.

A championship dirt-track race consists of 20 races. Since only four racers compete at one time, this lets all riders race each other.

The best team in dirt-track racing was Harley-Davidson's racing team of the 1920s and 1930s. The team was nicknamed the

25

A dirt-track race is close all the way up to the finish line.

Wrecking Crew because the riders beat all the other racing motorcycles.

Grand National Racing

Dirt-track racing is held mainly in the United States. The American Motorcyclist

Association (AMA) controls the dirt-track races called the Grand National series.

Top riders such as Chris Carr, Ricky Graham, and Scott Parker can round the dirt track at speeds above 130 miles (208 kilometers) per hour.

Motocross races
take place on
natural terrain.

Chapter 7

Motocross Racing

In the 1930s, motocross racing developed from dirt-track racing. During that time, people started riding Harley-Davidson and Indian racing motorcycles on off-road courses.

The Track

Today, motocross tracks are built on natural terrain. Every track is unique. Courses are challenging. Riders often have to deal with steep hills, tall jumps, and even trees.

Regulation motocross tracks are between .5 and 2 miles (.8 and 3.2 kilometers) long.

The Cycles

The motocross tracks are very rough. Motocross cycles must be lighter and have better **suspension** or shock absorbers.

Motocross cycles have small **two-stroke** engines of 125cc, 250cc, and 500cc. They are light but still give the motorcycle a lot of power.

The 16-inch (41-centimeter) wheels are held in place by **telescopic fork legs** and a **rear swing arm** with one or two shock absorbers. The shock absorbers dampen the jolts. It is important to soften landings after riding off large jumps.

The Race

A motocross race, or **moto**, is held over a set distance (such as five laps) or a set time (15 minutes).

Top speed for a motocross bike is around 75 miles (120 kilometers) per hour.

In motocross, riders jump high into the air. They speed down steep hills. Bikes rocket through the **berms**.

Berms and Doubles

Mounds of banked dirt, called berms, shape the course. Motocross riders use the berms to make sharp turns. The slope of the berms holds the wheels under the bike.

A special challenge for the motocrosser is "the double." A double is a pair of jumps. They can be taken in one single jump, if the racer goes fast enough. If the bike does not quite clear the second jump, a painful fall is sure to result.

Motocross racing involves dangerous obstacles, including trees.

Two riders jockey for position in a
stadium supercross event.

Chapter 8

Supercross Racing

Supercross is a style of motocross held in a stadium so the fans can easily see all of the race. Track builders bring dirt into the stadium and make jumps, bumps, and berms.

The Track

Supercross tracks are different from standard motocross tracks. They have more jumps and the turns are tighter. And they do not have natural obstacles such as steep hills and trees.

The length of the supercross track depends on the size of the stadium the race is held in.

The Cycles

Supercross riders use motocross bikes. Supercross races are divided into classes based on engine size. The classes are 125cc and 250cc engine sizes. (The 500cc motocross cycles are too large and heavy for the tight supercross tracks.)

The Race

A supercross race has sharp, twisting turns, short **straightaways**, and challenging jumps.

Supercross tracks are much smaller than motocross tracks. Top speeds are a bit slower. On the fastest part of the track, supercross bikes reach 65 miles (105 kilometers) per hour.

To ride in a supercross race, a rider must be good at turns and jumps.

Supercross Superstar

The superstar of supercross is Jeremy McGrath. In 1993, when he was only 21 years old, he was the fastest supercross racer around. He had been racing in motocross since he was in high school.

Supercross riders tackle a series of challenging jumps.

McGrath was a rookie when he entered supercross in 1993. But he did not just win the first series. He won almost every race he entered. He won 10 races his first season, including four in a row on his 250cc Honda.

This road-racing motorcycle is lifted into midair by its powerful engine.

Chapter 9

Road Racing

After motordrome racing was declared too dangerous, motorcycle races were held on public roads. The roads were simply blocked off for each event.

The Track

These races were also very dangerous. Special racetracks were soon built for racing cars and motorcycles on pavement. Some of the earliest tracks included Watkins Glen in New York; Road America in Elkhart Lake, Wisconsin; and Daytona International

Speedway in Daytona Beach, Florida, built in 1959.

The Cycles

Road-racing motorcycles are different from dirt-trackers or motocross cycles. The engines are much larger, heavier, and more powerful. Their top speeds are much faster. On the straightaways, speeds up to 170 miles (274 kilometers) per hour are common.

A road racer rockets down a straightaway.

Before a race, a road racer cleans the rear tire of the motorcycle by doing a "burnout."

Most road racing motorcycles have fiberglass **fairings**. Fairings streamline the motorcycle. This lets it cut through the air and go even faster.

Drag racer Mac Thrasher jumps off the starting line.

Chapter 10

Drag Racing

Drag racing is the simplest form of motorcycle racing. The track is short and the race lasts only a few seconds.

The Track

Drag-racing tracks are simple, straight stretches of pavement. The track is .25 mile (.4 kilometer) long.

Drag motorcycles reach such high speeds that racers need a section twice as long as the track to slow down.

A lighted pole called the Christmas tree signals the start of a drag race.

The Cycles

Drag-racing motorcycles are built for top speed. They have huge engines, 1500cc and more. Some even use two engines hooked together.

The Race

Drag racers line up their cycles at the start and do **burn-outs**. Before they race, they spin the rear tire on the pavement until it is hot. A burn-out cleans the tire and makes it stick to the track better.

After burn-outs, the racers wait for the signal. They watch a lighted pole called the **Christmas tree**.

Finally, the light turns from red to yellow to green. Racers roar their engines to top speed and blast off down the track. The first one to the end wins. Because drag racers reach such high speeds, they use parachutes to slow down.

Some of the fastest drag racers can run at more than 180 miles (290 kilometers) per hour. The entire race has an **elapsed time**, or ET, of less than 8 seconds!

Drag racer Happy Ring will reach 180 miles (290 kilometers) per hour by the time he reaches the finish.

Glossary

acceleration–the process of going faster

berm–a sloped mound of dirt that makes up a turn for motocross cycles

broadside–the act of leaning a motorcycle through the turn while balancing with an outstretched leg

chassis–the sturdy frame that holds the pieces of an engine together

checkered flag–the flag used to signal the end of a race

Christmas tree–a lighted pole in drag racing that starts the race

elapsed time–the length of time it takes for a competitor to finish a race

fairing–a fiberglass shell that streamlines a motorcycle

full-face helmet–a shielded helmet that covers the entire head

horsepower–a measurement of engine power

moto–one of a series of motocross races

motordrome–a rounded motorcycle racing track

purse–the prize money that racers are awarded for winning a race

rear swing arm–a metal, wishbone-shaped piece that holds the rear wheel and suspension

riding leathers–the leather or heavy nylon pants that motorcycle riders wear

steward–a referee who uses flags to direct a race

straightaway–a straight section of a race track

suspension–a system of shock absorbers by which the wheels are connected to the chassis

telescopic fork leg–(part of the suspension) pieces that connect the front wheels to the chassis

two-stroke engine–a simple, lightweight, high-speed engine

velodrome–a rounded bicycle racing track

WFO (wide full open)–describes racing a machine at top speed

To Learn More

Armitage, Barry. *Motorcycles!* New York: Sterling, 1988.

Baumann, Elwood D. *An Album of Motorcycles and Motorcycle Racing.* New York: F. Watts, 1982.

Kahaner, Ellen. *Motorcycles.* Mankato, MN: Capstone Press, 1991.

Stewart, Gail. *Motorcycle Racing.* Mankato, MN: Crestwood House, 1988.

Index

American Motorcyclist
  Association 26-27

berm, 30, 31, 33
bicycles, 8
boots, 19, 20-21
brakes, 24
broadside, 25
burn-outs, 42

Carr, Chris, 27
chassis, 24
Christmas tree, 43

Daimler, Gottlieb, 7
dirt track, 5, 23, 24;
  motorcycles, 24, 38;
  racing, 16, 19, 20-21,
  23-27
"double, the," 31
drag racing, 41-43;
  motorcycles, 42, 43;
  tracks, 41, 43

engines, 7, 8, 24, 30,
  34, 38, 42

gloves, 19, 20
Graham, Ricky, 27
Grand National Racing,
  27

Harley-Davidson, 8,
  24, 25, 29
Hedstrom, Oscar, 8
helmets, 19, 21
Hendee, George, 8

Indian, 8, 29

jumps, 29, 30, 31, 33, 34

McGrath, Jeremy, 34-35
motocross motorcycles,
  30, 34, 38; racing, 16,
  19, 20-21, 29-31;
  tracks, 29

Parker, Scott, 27
pavement, 5, 13, 20, 37, 41
purse, 24

riding leathers, 19-20
road racing, 13, 20, 37; motorcycles, 24, 38-39; tracks, 37
speeds, 5, 8, 11, 27, 30, 34, 38, 41, 42, 43

supercross
motorcycles, 34; racing, 16, 19, 20-21, 33-35; tracks, 33, 34
suspension, 30

turns, 5, 13, 16, 20, 23, 25, 31, 33, 34

Wrecking Crew, 26

Photo Credits:
Allsport: cover, pp. 10, 14-15, 36, 38, 39; Chris Bense: pp. 4, 28; American Motorcyclist Association: pp.6, 9, 22, 25, 26; Duomo: pp. 12, 16, 18, 32, 35; Cheryl Blair: p. 31; All-Harley Drag Association: pp. 40, 42, 43.